SUNKEN TREASURE
by Gail Gibbons

Thomas Y. Crowell   New York

Library of Congress Cataloging-in-Publication Data
Gibbons, Gail.
   Sunken treasure / by Gail Gibbons. — 1st ed.
      p.   cm.
   Summary: Describes the many-years-long search for the treasure that went down
with the *Atocha*, a Spanish galleon sunk off Florida in a hurricane in 1622.
   ISBN 0-690-04734-7 : $ ISBN 0-690-04736-3 (lib. bdg.) : $
   1. Nuestra Señora de Atocha (Ship)—Juvenile literature.   2. Treasure-trove—
Florida—Juvenile literature.   [1. Nuestra Señora de Atocha (Ship)
2. Buried treasure.]   I. Title.
G530.N83G5   1988
917.59′41—dc19   87-30114
                                                          CIP
                                                          AC

Special thanks to Chris Paterson for making me aware of the discovery of the
Atocha; and to Don Kincaid, Greg Wareham, Taffi Fisher Quesada, and
Kathryn Simpson of Treasure Salvors, Inc., Key West, FL; Dana Thayer of the Whydah
Management Co., Inc., NY; Charles Haas of the Titanic Historical Society, Inc., NJ;
and Nancy Green of Woods Hole Oceanographic Institution, MA.

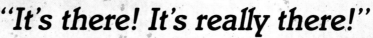

"It's there! It's really there!"

The rotting hull of a ship has been found on the ocean floor. Within the wreck lies a fabulous treasure.

The story of each underwater treasure hunt is different, but each goes back to the same beginning...the sinking of a ship. The story of the hunt for the *Nuestra Señora de Atocha*, a Spanish galleon, begins the same way.

THE ATOCHA

The Sinking

It is 1622. The *Atocha*, with its fleet of sister ships, makes its way back from South America to Spain. The *Atocha* is a treasure ship, laden with gold, jewels, silver bars, and thousands of coins.

The fleet makes a stop in Cuba and then sets off again. As the ships near Florida, a hurricane gathers strength.

Wind rips at the *Atocha*'s sails. Spray washes across the deck. The 265 people aboard the ship are terrified. Suddenly, a huge wave lifts the ship and throws it against a reef.

The hull breaks open, and the *Atocha*—
along with several of its sister ships—sinks
beneath the waves. All but five aboard the
Atocha drown.

The Search

Spain wants its treasure back. Search ships are sent out. They find one of the *Atocha's* sister ships, the *Santa Margarita*, and salvage begins. Sponge and pearl divers bring some of the *Santa Margarita's* treasure to the surface.

But the *Atocha* cannot be found.

Hundreds of years go by. The *Atocha* is almost forgotten. Storms and strong sea currents scatter its treasure for miles along the ocean floor. The ship slowly rots and breaks into pieces. Sand covers the remains.

In the early 1960's, a new search begins.
A man named Mel Fisher has read about
the *Atocha*. He is determined to find
the lost treasure ship. He will need boats,
crew, and equipment. Investors provide
the money, and the venture gets under way.

Search boats go to where it is believed
the *Atocha* went down.

The side-scan sonar takes readings of the ocean floor.

The magnetometer detects metal objects.

The boats are fitted with modern equipment for exploring the ocean bottom.

When the instruments register a "hit," divers go down to investigate. They keep in view of each other and regularly check their air supplies.

air tank

The underwater metal detector locates metal objects, too.

mailboxes

Large elbow-shaped pipes, called
mailboxes, are swung into place.
The mailboxes are Mel Fisher's invention.
The whirling of the boat's propellers forces
water through the mailboxes, blowing large
holes in the sand. If anything is buried,
it will be uncovered.

But only litter is found—nothing of value,
nothing from the *Atocha*.

Where should they look next?

Mel Fisher asks for help from Eugene Lyon, an expert who can translate old Spanish documents. Lyon looks through stacks of shipping records from the 1600's. The work takes years.

Finally, in 1970, he finds a clue! He discovers new evidence pointing to where the *Atocha* sank—a new area 100 miles away from where the team has been looking. Lyon also finds a cargo list that tells what the *Atocha* was carrying.

old area

new area

A search boat moves to the new location.
In 1971, a huge galleon anchor, several muskets, and gold bars and chains are found. But are they from the *Atocha*? There is no way to prove it.

Two years later, three heavy silver bars are recovered. The bars with their markings match up with the *Atocha's* cargo list. Now they have proof!

Then, in 1975, the *Atocha*'s bronze cannons are found. The crew believe they are getting closer to the mother lode...the main treasure of the ship.

But they are wrong. Day after day they search the huge area. Many more years go by. Crew members leave and new ones sign on. When the money runs out, new investors must be found.

The Find

1985. The crew go back and search a site they had searched years ago. And then it happens—a big "hit" registers on their equipment. Divers go down.

"We found it! The mother lode!"

Mel Fisher's twenty-year search is finally over. Resting on the ocean floor, 55 feet below, is the *Atocha*'s fabled treasure— glinting gold bars, jewelry, gold and silver coins, and other precious finds. Nearly all the listed cargo is there, and more— some treasure must have been smuggled aboard.

The Recording

The crew works with a marine archaeologist, Duncan Mathewson. He insists that the mother lode not be disturbed. A grid of plastic pipes is laid over the site.

underwater camera

The divers take pictures and make drawings square by square. Each square of the grid is numbered. That way the exact position of each timber, coin, and artifact is recorded.

Later, archaeologists and historians will use this information to learn about times past.

underwater slate

grid marker number 24

25

The Salvage

Now the treasure can be brought to the surface. Salvage boats are moved in. Divers descend and crew members lower baskets over the side to them.

The divers gently fan the sand with their hands and use an airlift to carefully suck it away.

airlift

As treasure is recovered, other artifacts are exposed underneath. Each piece of treasure must be accounted for. Again, everything found is sketched and photographed.

One after another, baskets full of treasure are raised to the surface.

Each day the work continues...dive after dive after dive. More treasure is recovered from the deep. It is hard work and can be done only in good weather.

The salvage goes on for weeks, months, and years.

Restoration and Preservation

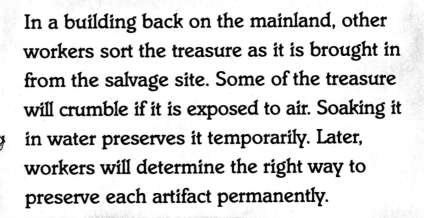

In a building back on the mainland, other workers sort the treasure as it is brought in from the salvage site. Some of the treasure will crumble if it is exposed to air. Soaking it in water preserves it temporarily. Later, workers will determine the right way to preserve each artifact permanently.

Silver coins are put into chemical baths to clean and restore them. In one or two days they will look like new.

Silver bars soak in chemical baths, too, but they will take longer to clean. They are bigger. The gold from the *Atocha* is already shiny—gold never loses its luster.

There were many pottery storage jars on board the *Atocha*. Amazingly, some are recovered whole. Other jars had been shattered and now must be pieced together again.

Cataloging

Cataloging of the *Atocha*'s treasure is done in several ways:

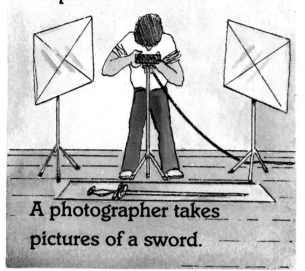

A photographer takes pictures of a sword.

Coins are scanned by a computer, and an exact description of each one is stored in the computer's memory.

An artist draws pictures of a gold plate and an emerald-studded necklace.

This kind of careful cataloging provides a valuable record for the future.

Distribution

Some of the treasure will go to museums.

Some will go to the investors and some will go to the crew. All of them made it possible for Mel Fisher's long search to continue. A computer works out what each one's fair share will be.

The treasure of the *Nuestra Señora de Atocha* is valued at hundreds of millions of dollars...a very wealthy treasure ship indeed!

The wreck and its artifacts will be studied by historians and archaeologists for years to come. Their discoveries will enrich our knowledge of the past. This will be the second treasure of the *Atocha*.

OTHER FAMOUS TREASURE HUNTS
THE MARY ROSE • an English warship

The Sinking

In 1545, the *Mary Rose*, the pride of Henry VIII's fleet, set sail to do battle against the French. She never fired a shot. Overloaded with guns and armed men, she sank off the coast of England.

The Search

In 1965, a group of British historians undertook a search for the *Mary Rose*. They knew approximately where she had gone down, but over the centuries she had been buried in sand and silt.

The Find

Two years later the *Mary Rose* was found.

The Salvage

For years divers salvaged at the site. Then, in 1982, modern equipment was used to raise the hull of the ship.

Restoration & Preservation

A special museum was built to house the hull of the *Mary Rose*. The hull must be constantly sprayed with a cold-water mist to keep the wood from disintegrating. Eventually, a waxy preserving solution will be added to the mist. The process of preservation will be completed in 2001.

Learning About the Past

The layers of mud that had settled on the *Mary Rose* preserved fragile pieces of clothing, shoes and boots. From these we know what sailors wore in 16th-century England.

By studying the hull, historians learned about shipbuilding methods at that time.

THE VASA · a Swedish warship

The Sinking

1628. The *Vasa* capsized in Stockholm's harbor on her maiden voyage. The ship was badly designed—it was top-heavy.

The Search

In 1953, after years of studying maps and documents, a former Swedish Navy officer organized a search.

The Find

In 1956 the wreck of the *Vasa* was found.

The Salvage

Swedish Navy divers dug tunnels under the hull and ran heavy cables through them. Then the *Vasa* was pulled to shallow water. There it was made watertight, pumped dry, and floated back to drydock.

Restoration & Preservation

Today the *Vasa* is in a museum. Jets of steam and chemicals continually spray the hull to keep it from warping.

Learning About the Past

Food found preserved in storage containers from the *Vasa* showed what seamen ate aboard ship in the 1600's.

Historians studied the wreck to learn about old Swedish shipbuilding methods.

THE WHYDAH • a pirate ship

The Sinking

The *Whydah* ran aground off Cape Cod, Massachusetts, in 1717.

The Search

In 1982, a salvage expert began searching for the *Whydah* using a magnetometer and a side-scan sonar.

The Find

After three years, the search crew succeeded in locating the wreck.

The Salvage

Using mailboxes to clear away sand, divers uncovered valuable treasure and began raising it to the surface.

Restoration & Preservation

Silver coins and other pirate plunder are being cleaned and preserved by the same methods used to protect the *Atocha*'s treasure.

Learning About the Past

The 200-pound bronze bell from the ship was found. On it were the words THE WHYDAH GALLY—1716. This proved the wreck was the legendary pirate ship. It is believed that the *Whydah* is the first pirate ship ever to be salvaged.

THE TITANIC • a luxury liner

The Sinking

On its first voyage from England to America, in 1912, the *Titanic* struck an iceberg off the coast of Nova Scotia and sank. More than 1500 passengers and crew members lost their lives.

The Search

Over the years many separate searches failed to locate the *Titanic*. It lay in very deep water, 12,500 feet down. In 1981, an international team sponsored by Woods Hole Oceanographic Institute began a new search. Towing a sonar and video platform called *Argo*, they were able to make continuous videotapes of the ocean floor.

The Find

1986. The team located the *Titanic* and used an underwater craft named *Alvin*, along with its robot *Jason Jr.*, to explore the wreck.

The Salvage

After the find, many people argued that the *Titanic* should be left undisturbed as a memorial to those who lost their lives. Nevertheless, in 1987 salvage operations began, and divers carried more than 800 artifacts to the surface.

Learning About the Past

It had been thought that a gash was torn in the *Titanic*'s hull when it hit the iceberg. But the *Alvin* explorations found no gash. Scientists now believe the collision may have buckled plates in the ship's hull, allowing water to pour in.

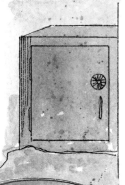

THE HISTORY OF DIVING

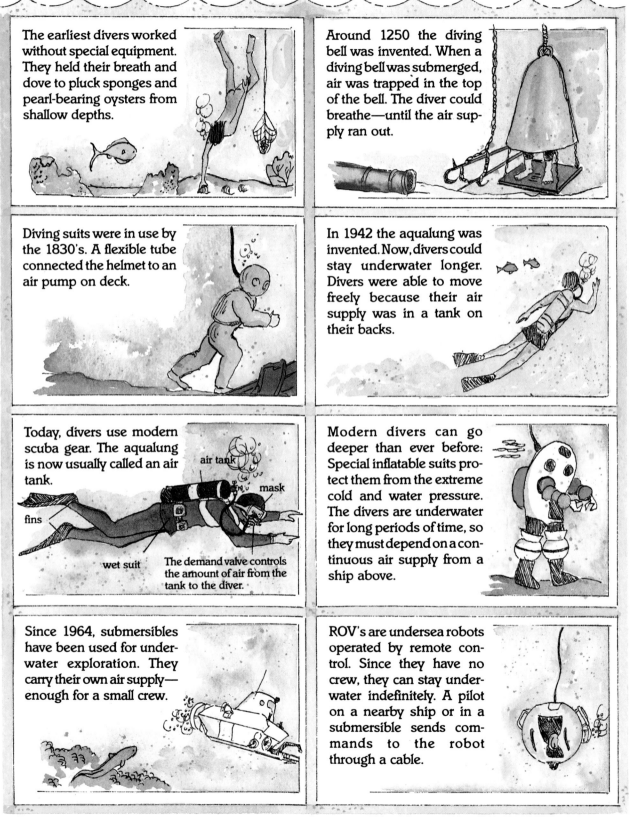

The earliest divers worked without special equipment. They held their breath and dove to pluck sponges and pearl-bearing oysters from shallow depths.

Around 1250 the diving bell was invented. When a diving bell was submerged, air was trapped in the top of the bell. The diver could breathe—until the air supply ran out.

Diving suits were in use by the 1830's. A flexible tube connected the helmet to an air pump on deck.

In 1942 the aqualung was invented. Now, divers could stay underwater longer. Divers were able to move freely because their air supply was in a tank on their backs.

Today, divers use modern scuba gear. The aqualung is now usually called an air tank.

air tank

mask

fins

wet suit

The demand valve controls the amount of air from the tank to the diver.

Modern divers can go deeper than ever before: Special inflatable suits protect them from the extreme cold and water pressure. The divers are underwater for long periods of time, so they must depend on a continuous air supply from a ship above.

Since 1964, submersibles have been used for underwater exploration. They carry their own air supply—enough for a small crew.

ROV's are undersea robots operated by remote control. Since they have no crew, they can stay underwater indefinitely. A pilot on a nearby ship or in a submersible sends commands to the robot through a cable.